YOUTH BIBLE STUDY GUIDE

Hunger, Poverty and Justice

Youth Bible Study Guides

Sexuality

Following God

Image and Self-Esteem

Peer Pressure

Father God

Jesus Christ and the Holy Spirit

Sin, Forgiveness and Eternal Life

Church, Prayer and Worship

Sharing Your Faith

Tough Times

Money and Giving

Hunger, Poverty and Justice

YOUTH BIBLE STUDY GUIDE

Hunger, Poverty and Justice

COMPILED AND WRITTEN BY
CHIP AND HELEN KENDALL

Authentic

Those who help the poor succeed will get many blessings. When trouble comes, the Lord will save them. The Lord will protect them and save their lives. He will bless them in this land. He will not let their enemies harm them.
(Psalm 41:1–2)

Chip and Helen Kendall are Creative Arts Pastors at Audacious Church, Manchester, and also love spending as much time as possible with their kids, Cole, Eden and Elliot. They currently reside in Stockport, England and they still have trouble understanding each other's accents.

Chip tours the world, fronting the Chip Kendall Band. His album *Holy Freaks* and first book *The Mind of chipK: Enter at Your Own Risk* have helped loads of young people grow in their faith. He's also the driving force behind a new youth media movement called MYvoice with Cross Rhythms, as well as being a regular presenter on GodTV. All of these jobs continue to pave the way for him to speak at events everywhere. www.chipkendall.com

After working for ten years as a dancer and tour/bookings manager, Helen now juggles looking after the kids with her work at Audacious Church helping to develop dance and all things creative. She also enjoys doing some writing and project management. Helen loves the variety in her life, and no two days are ever the same.

Thank Yous

Massive thanks to Malcolm Down, Liz Williams and the rest of the gang at Authentic Media for giving us the opportunity to work on these study guides . . . it's been a blast. Thanks to everyone at Audacious Church for being an amazing church family. Thanks to Julian, Tony and Ben for chatting to Helen for this book. Thanks to lovely Lucy West for the fantastic photos. To everyone who talked to Chip for the 'people clips', thanks for your honesty and willingness to put up with the quirky questions. A really huge thank you to Brian and Norma Wilson for their 'hidden pearls' of wisdom. We loved your perspective on things. Finally, big thanks to all the authors whose work we have used in this book. You are an inspiration.

CONTENTS

INSTRUCTIONS

The book you're holding in your hands is a study guide. It's a compilation of extracts from lots of other books written about this subject. It might not make you the world's expert on the subject, but it should give you lots of useful information and, even better, it should give you some idea of what the Bible has to say about . . . HUNGER, POVERTY AND JUSTICE.

What is a 'reaction box'?

Throughout the book, you'll find these helpful little reaction boxes. We've added them so that you can decide for yourself what you think about what you've just read. Here's what one should look like once you've filled it in:

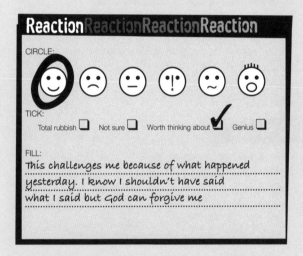

Reaction Reaction Reaction Reaction

CIRCLE:

TICK:
Total rubbish ☐   Not sure ☐   Worth thinking about ✓   Genius ☐

FILL:
This challenges me because of what happened
yesterday. I know I shouldn't have said
what I said but God can forgive me

Pretty simple really . . .

Circle the face that reflects how you feel about it.

Tick the box that shows what you think about it.

Fill in any thoughts you have about what you've learned on the lines provided.

What are 'people clips'?

Just so you don't get too bored, we've added a bunch of 'people clips' to each study guide. These are people just like you, who were happy for us to pick their brains about various related topics. Who knows? Maybe you'll find someone you recognize.

What are 'hidden pearls'?

Everyone needs some good old-fashioned 'grandparently' advice, so we collected some pearls of wisdom from our friends Brian and Norma Wilson, which you can find scattered throughout the book.

What is a 'reality check'?

Finally, throughout the book you will come across sections called 'reality check'. These should provide a chance for you to apply what you've been learning to your own life experiences.

Other than that, the only rule that applies when reading this book is that you HAVE FUN! So start reading.

Chip & Helen

Introduction

(Zechariah 7:9)

What do you have a right to? A roof over your head? Food to eat? The right to a fair trial? Quality medical attention if you are ill? Respect? An education? Voting? A living wage? Freedom? In our society we have a lot of rights, but have you ever thought how quickly your life would change if someone took even one of your rights away? What if today a new law came in to say that everyone between the ages of 14 and 20 could only earn £2 per hour no matter what job they did, to help businesses lower their wage bill? Or what if suddenly it was decided that girls were not allowed to go to school? Or what if your house and everything your family owned was destroyed in a flood and you had to go and live in a tent in a refugee camp?

Often when we watch the news and see desperate people walking miles for food, carrying all their belongings on their backs or shouting and screaming for help, we think to ourselves, 'Well, they aren't like us, so it's not as bad for them.' But then we realize that's just not true. Only a few things would need to change for us to be in the same place as those desperate people; just a few things would need to change and that could be you or me. These are often just people whose rights have been taken away, people whose security has been taken away, people who have suffered an injustice.

Jesus had a lot of time for the poor and the Bible has a lot to say about justice and how we should look after those who are not as fortunate as us. We really hope this book will help you understand a bit about God's heart for the poor and the hungry and help you figure out how you can take a stand for justice.

Hunger and Poverty

Great blessings belong to those who know
  they are spiritually in need.
  God's kingdom belongs to them.
Great blessings belong to those who are sad now.
  God will comfort them.
Great blessings belong to those who are humble.
  They will be given the land God promised.
Great blessings belong to those who want to do right
  more than anything else.
  God will fully satisfy them.
Great blessings belong to those who show mercy to others.
  Mercy will be given to them.
Great blessings belong to those whose thoughts are pure.
  They will be with God.
Great blessings belong to those who work to bring peace.
  God will call them his sons and daughters.
Great blessings belong to those who suffer persecution
  for doing what is right.
  God's kingdom belongs to them.

(Matthew 5:3–10)

First up

Messed up are those who are poor.
　They miss out on all the good things in life.
Annoying are those who are sad.
　They should get over it and have a good time.
Time-wasting are the humble.
　They should push themselves forward and they would get what
　they want quicker.
Boring are those who try to get justice.
　They go on and on about issues and aren't much fun to be around.
Stupid are those who put others in front of themselves.
　They will never get ahead.
Prudish are those who stay pure.
　Why not mess around and have a bit of fun?
Tired-out are those who work to try and bring peace in the world.
　They should just make sure they are happy themselves and
　then relax.
Unfashionable are those who do good.
　They should be controversial as it's more likely to get
　them famous!

Does the lists of truths in Matthew 5:3–10 or the list above more accurately reflect your approach to life, if you are honest? Are you humble? Do you even have any time for humble people? Do you show mercy to others or are you too busy trying to get ahead to notice others? Do you hunger and thirst for justice, or do you just turn a blind eye to the oppressed people in the world because you are OK? Have you ever stood up for what is right even if it meant getting into trouble yourself?

It is very easy to find yourself living by the set of values above, rather than the values set out in the Bible. Our society tells us to just look after

I ♥ #1

number one. It tells us that poor people are probably that way because they are just lazy or corrupt. It tells us to push others down rather than helping them up. Go to www.biblegateway.com and type 'poor' into the keyword search. You will find pages and pages of references to the poor and hungry. The main impression you get as you check out some of the verses is of God's mercy and love for the poor. How he longs to lift them out of their distress and help them. For example:

> He raises the poor from the dust, and he takes away their sadness. He makes them important and seats them with princes and at the places for honoured guests. The LORD made the whole world, and the whole world belongs to him.

(1 Samuel 2:8)

The Bible also has a lot to say about what our response to the poor and needy should be:

> When you are living in the land the LORD your God is giving you, there might be some poor people living among you. You must not be selfish. You must not refuse to give help to them.

(Deuteronomy 15:7)

There are also loads of examples in the Bible of people crying out to God to look after the poor, like David in Psalms pleading:

> Defend the poor and orphans. Protect the rights of the poor.

(Psalm 82:3)

This Life Lesson is all about hunger and poverty because the Bible has loads to say about the poor and our response to them. We hope this will help you make a decision to live by the values spelled out by God rather than by everyone else.

Make the First Last

> He reached out his arm and showed his power.
> He scattered those who think they are better than anyone else.
> He brought down rulers from their thrones
> and raised up the humble people.
> He filled the hungry with good things,
> but he sent the rich away with nothing.

(Luke 1:51–53)

Mary is rejoicing in the upside-down world of the kingdom of God.

We still live in a world where 'might is right' and the gap is still growing between rich and poor. In what ways are we seeking to turn the world upside-down? In what ways are we being counter-cultural? Do we challenge those who are using power to wield influence? Do we allow people to use their mood or threat of a mood to influence decision-making?

Somehow we are attracted to those who have most earthly power. We seem to believe that certain people might just do us a favour or will sprinkle some 'magic dust' on us. You can see this at meetings where politicians are present. Everyone hovers around them, hoping for some power to rub off. But you can also see this in a playground, where people hover around the person with the most power. They may be the loudest, the cheekiest, the rudest or the strongest. This isn't the way of things in God's kingdom. In his kingdom, the 'last shall be first' and the 'meek will inherit the earth', because they haven't grabbed and controlled it.

TODAY RESOLVE TO STRIKE A BLOW FOR THE UNDERDOG. Stand up for the guy or girl who is normally the brunt of the class jokes. Make way in the queue for the mother struggling with her kids. Take time to chat to the ancillary staff in your school.

I heard the author Stuart Briscoe crystallize some of this kingdom thinking recently. He said, 'We express the kingdom when we do what is good instead of what is comfortable, when we do what is right instead of what is profitable, and when we stand by what is true rather than what is popular.' Weigh up some of your recent decisions on these three axes, and see how you're doing . . .

My mate Colin impresses me with his attitude to business. On meeting a new boss, he always tells them, 'I won't lie for you.' But he follows it with, 'And that's a good thing, because it means I won't lie to you, either.'

Andy Flannagan, *God 360°*, Authentic Media and Spring Harvest Publishing, 2006

Reaction Reaction Reaction Reaction

CIRCLE:

😊 😦 😐 😮 😕 😲

TICK:

Total rubbish ☐   Not sure ☐   Worth thinking about ☐   Genius ☐

FILL:

....

....

....

....

Hidden pearls

We try to support organizations that help the poor. I was out in India during the war, so I saw poverty first hand, I saw people hungry. A lot of the wealthy people I came across out there didn't seem to bother about the local poor. In the forces we often gave to the poor people who were begging.

Hunger Games

Chip Talks

Jakob's whole life felt empty. His home was empty. His heart was empty. His pockets were empty. And worst of all, his stomach was empty. He hadn't eaten anything for two days, and he was starting to feel desperate.

'Jakob!' It was Sophie, one of his friends from school. 'I haven't seen you for a while. You OK?' she asked.

'Yeah, I'm alright . . . I guess,' he replied.

In reality, Jakob was hurting. He needed help, and he knew it. But his pride was bigger than his ability to ask for it. So he would play the game of keeping up appearances and spend every last penny on the latest brands in order to hide the difficult truth that **ON THE INSIDE, HE WAS WASTING AWAY**.

'Alright then,' Sophie turned to go. But after walking a few paces in the opposite direction, she turned back around. 'Wait a sec . . .'

Secretly, Jakob was happy that Sophie cared enough to carry on the conversation. Most of his friends were so self-obsessed and worried about what others thought of them that they never took the time to really connect with him.

Sophie carried on, 'I don't mean to sound weird or anything, but . . . well . . . it's just that . . . you already know that I go to church, right? Well, last Sunday I felt that God spoke to me about you while I was praying. And I just want to say that if you ever need anything, please don't be afraid to ask.'

Jakob couldn't believe what he was hearing. Maybe it was time to tell someone what was really going on . . .

Love each other as your own family. And try to be the first in
giving honour to each other ... Live together in peace with
each other. Don't be proud, but be willing to be friends with
people who are not important to others. Don't think of
yourself as smarter than everyone else.

(Romans 12:10,16)

God is the one who gives seed to those who plant, and he gives
bread for food. And God will give you spiritual seed and make
that seed grow. He will produce a great harvest from your
goodness.

(2 Corinthians 9:10)

Consider . . .

- We never know who might be suffering in silence. You can't judge
  a book by its cover. Why not take a few minutes to pray and ask
  Jesus if there is a 'Jakob' in your life?

- There are many young people living beneath the poverty line,
  even in this country. Consider finding out more by supporting a
  local charity.

- Jesus refers to himself as the 'bread of life'. What are some
  practical ways that we can enjoy him and even share him with
  others?

Reaction Reaction Reaction Reaction

CIRCLE:

☺ ☹ 😐 😯 😌 😲

TICK:

Total rubbish ☐   Not sure ☐   Worth thinking about ☐   Genius ☐

FILL:

....
....
....
....

Name: **Dannielle Norman**

Age: **20**

Town: **Manchester/Basingstoke**

Occupation: **PR and Fundraising Intern with The Message Trust**

Favourite sport

I like to watch gymnastics, but I like to horse ride, dance and use the free weights at the gym.

If you could enter any event in the Olympics what would it be?

Gymnastics, if I could do it! They're very disciplined. People underestimate the control gymnasts have.

Which colour did God invent first?

Blue is the obvious one, but I'd like to think it was green – that's my favourite colour.

Any siblings?

Two beautiful sisters. I have middle child syndrome.

What would you say to your younger sister about the topic of justice?

We've got it so easy, the least we can do is pray. At best we can sacrifice everything we have for the cause.

What was Jesus' approach to poverty?

Um, I can't say I know too much, but I can say that he LOVES everyone, first and foremost. Loving people is the start of transformation.

chipK's mind

You don't have to search very hard in God's Word to find out that his heart beats for the poor. King David started life as a grubby shepherd boy. Joseph was sold into slavery by his jealous brothers. John the Baptist survived on sticky-grasshopper-pudding for much of his life. Even Jesus himself was poor enough to be born in an extremely unhygienic stable. Yet all of these people were used by God to change the course of history.

I came face to face with blatant poverty while on a ministry trip with my family to Romania. First off, the entire country seemed to smell of hideous body odour. Secondly, I just about passed out after being directed towards a communal outhouse at the back of a broken-down gas station to relieve myself. The stench was so horrific I had to hold my breath, and even still, I could literally taste it on my tongue. Thirdly, I'll never forget stopping at some traffic lights and watching as three sad little kids came over to our car and started wiping our windscreen with dirty, oily rags. They stared longingly at us through big hungry eyes as they proceeded to 'clean' our car, actually making it dirtier than it already was! We didn't have any money in their currency yet, so my mom rummaged around desperately and found a small pack of cookies. When she handed it to them through her window, their huge eyes widened even further as if she was handing them the greatest gift they'd ever been given. We watched them as they ran off and formed a huddle in order to divvy up their new-found spoils – a crummy handful of cookies.

Jesus said that the poor would always be with us. But how will we choose to treat them? **CAN WE REALLY GET AWAY WITH IGNORING THE HOMELESS PERSON ON THE HIGH STREET?** What would Jesus do? If you ask me, it's time to stop judging and start loving.

God's mind

'You will always have those who are poor with you. But you will not always have me.'
(John 12:8)

'Then those people will answer, "Lord, when did we see you hungry or thirsty? When did we see you without a place to stay? When did we see you without clothes or sick or in prison? When did we see any of this and not help you?" The king will answer, "The truth is, anything you refused to do for any of my people here, you refused to do for me." Then these evil people will go away to be punished forever. But the godly people will go and enjoy eternal life.'
(Matthew 25:44–46)

Then Jesus said to the Pharisee who had invited him, 'When you give a lunch or a dinner, don't invite only your friends, brothers, relatives and rich neighbours. At another time they will pay you back by inviting you to eat with them. Instead, when you give a feast, invite the poor, the lame and the blind. Then you will have great blessings, because these people cannot pay you back. They have nothing.'
(Luke 14:12–14)

'The Spirit of the Lord is on me. He has chosen me to tell good news to the poor. He sent me to tell prisoners that they are free and to tell the blind that they can see again. He sent me to free those who have been treated badly and to announce that the time has come for the Lord to show his kindness.'
(Luke 4:18–19)

Story of the Good Samaritan
(Luke 10:30–35)

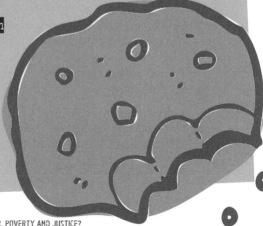

Your mind

When was the last time I helped out someone who was poor?

....

....

What is my first reaction to a homeless person on the high street?

....

....

Most people associate being poor with having no money. What are some other ways that people can be poor?

1...

2...

3...

What can I do this week to represent Jesus to someone who's poor?

....

....

Chip Kendall, *The Mind of chipK: Enter at Your Own Risk*, **Authentic Media, 2005**

Reaction ReactionReactionReaction

CIRCLE:

😊 😦 😐 😯 😌 😮

TICK:

Total rubbish ☐ Not sure ☐ Worth thinking about ☐ Genius ☐

FILL:

....

....

....

....

A-Teams

Helen talks

Audacious Church in Manchester runs a community outreach ministry called A-Teams. At the moment they are involved in welcoming more than fifty homeless people into the church every week for a hot meal. Other kinds of practical help like haircuts, help with filling in forms and clothes are also made available. On Fridays the team also goes out onto the streets of Manchester to help support people living rough there. A highlight in the church calendar is the huge Christmas banquet that the team puts on for the homeless, complete with table decorations, Christmas presents and crackers. Recently A-Teams invited seventy homeless people to eat in a buffet restaurant in Manchester, which was such a success it got coverage on the local news!

Julian Wolstencroft heads up the A-Teams ministry, so I asked him a few questions.

What was the inspiration for doing what you do with A-Teams?

From a personal point of view, my inspiration was listening to Tommy Barnett (founder of the Dream Centre in LA, www.dreamcenter.org) more than 10 years ago speak about how the church needs to just serve its city. No strings attached, just love and serve. Psalm 10 tells us that God listens to the cry of the afflicted.

LORD, you have heard what the poor want. Listen to their prayers, and do what they ask. Protect the orphans and those who have been hurt. Don't let powerful people drive us from our land!
(Psalm 10:17–18)

Are there any other Bible verses that encourage you to keep doing what you do?

'The truth is, anything you did for any of my people here, you also did for me.'
(Matthew 25:40)

What is the most difficult thing about working with the homeless?

The most difficult thing I would say is helping people to break the cycle they are in. They believe this is now their lot in life, having been on the streets for so long. Trying to get them to see there is a plan for them can be difficult. But when they break that cycle – get a flat, a job and everything that goes with it – that's amazing.

Do you come up against any prejudice or misconceptions?

There don't seem to be as many prejudices as there used to be. When we are out on the streets we find that people are generally sympathetic to the guys. There is, however, quite a big misconception around why people are homeless – not many people realize why it happens.

Do you think it is helpful to give money to people who are begging?

Whenever possible I would always encourage people to buy the person a meal or a sandwich. However, I would never say don't give them money. Who are we to judge them on how they spend that money?

If a young person reading this book wanted to do something to help the homeless, where should they start?

I would encourage them to find out what is happening in their town/city and go along and volunteer. Get involved and make a difference.

Read the following verses to get some more inspiration to help the poor:

- Deuteronomy 15:7–9

- James 2:1–9

Reaction Reaction Reaction Reaction

CIRCLE:

☺ ☹ 😐 😮 🙂 😲

TICK:

Total rubbish ☐   Not sure ☐   Worth thinking about ☐   Genius ☐

FILL:

....

....

....

....

Get Out

Jesus said to him, 'The foxes have holes to live in. The birds have nests. But the Son of Man has no place to rest.'
(Matthew 8:20)

How about spending a night sleeping rough? Perhaps you could arrange to do this with your youth group. Discover what it's like to be homeless, even for just one night. You will learn more and perhaps your heart will be softened more in eight hours than in a month of seminars on the subject. The cold, the loneliness and the vulnerability are merely concepts until you experience them.

On an earthly level, you could describe Jesus as homeless, but he was also displaced from his real home with his Father. Again Jesus shows his identification with those on the fringes of society. By sleeping rough you are identifying with millions of displaced people across our world who for various reasons have no roof over their heads – whether it is refugees from war in sub-Saharan Africa, street children in Central America, or the folks in your own town whose stories you only half believe.

Spend your sleepless moments praying for these situations. You may also want to identify with another sleepless night of prayer – that of Jesus in the Garden of Gethsemane. He may ask us, 'Could you watch and pray with me for just a few hours to kneel alongside the broken and dispossessed of my world?'

Andy Flannagan, *God 360°*, Spring Harvest and Authentic Media, 2006

ReactionReactionReactionReaction

CIRCLE:

😊 🙁 😐 😦 😕 😮

TICK:

Total rubbish ☐   Not sure ☐   Worth thinking about ☐   Genius ☐

FILL:

....

....

Heart for the broken

Helen talks

Have you ever passed a homeless person on the street and wondered what their story was, how they came to be in that position, and what you could do to help?

I recently chatted to a guy named Tony at our church to get his insight. Tony's mum left when he was 13 and his dad had a breakdown. After both parents remarried, Tony felt as if he was in the way and didn't fit with their new families. By the time he was 17 he'd started hanging round with some older lads and experimenting with drugs – weed first and eventually heroin – and soon he ended up addicted and homeless.

Tony talks

You've got to remember that back then there weren't the benefits you get now. There was no Jobseeker's Allowance or Housing Benefit, so I ended up having to beg. I would ask people for somewhere to stay, sleep on kitchen floors or at shelters or even in cupboards. I didn't sit down and beg – that wasn't me – but I would go up to people and ask them if they could spare a few pounds. Churches were always really good at helping out and I managed to get by. I was resourceful, and after a few years managed to get myself off the heroin by using cough medicine. After a number of years I got married and, again, a church took us in as a couple and really helped and supported us. They were great and we got really involved in the church.

It took a long time, but I managed to get off the drugs and start recovery. For a number of years everything was going well and life was good, but then the doctor told me that I'd contracted Hepatitis C and I had to go through a year of treatment like chemotherapy. This triggered another downward spiral and I ended up getting addicted to alcohol, my marriage fell apart and once again I became homeless. I drank myself into heart failure and the doctors told me I only had about a week to live.

But by the grace of God I'm still here. I did several detoxes with the help of medication, joined AA and now everything is different. I've got a place to live, a fiancée and I'm really involved in this church. God had me back because of his grace. I always believed in God throughout everything I've been through, but now I really understand his grace.

Now, I work with A-Teams, the homeless ministry here at church. I made myself available to God and he's used me and given me such a heart for the guys and girls on the streets. I honestly feel like they are my family, and when they hurt, I hurt too. There are some people you see again and again on the streets who seem to survive everything and there others who you think won't make it through the next few weeks, and they don't. God is using my past experience to help me connect. I'm working with addicts, I mentor homeless people for a local charity and I do a music group for another homeless charity.

It can sometimes be hard to know how to get involved with helping the homeless and broken, so I asked Tony where he felt was the best place to start.

Tony talks:

It's your heart. You've got to start with a heart for the homeless, for the broken. In fact not even just for homeless people. Even within church there will be people that won't say a word but are 'homeless' inside themselves and within their network of people. That heart of compassion and just being available to God is where I think you need to start. Some people are more equipped than others to deal with all the stuff that comes with working with homeless people. There's nothing that shocks me, as I've been there before, but we've also got people on the team who don't have my experience – people who have led normal lives; millionaires even – but they have a heart for the homeless. Get involved, give your time, either at your church or a local homeless charity and you will be blessed.

Read

So be sure to give to the poor. Don't hesitate to give to them, because the LORD your God will bless you for doing this good thing. He will bless you in all your work and in everything you do.
(Deuteronomy 15:10)

'So pay attention to what is inside. Give to the people who need help. Then you will be fully clean.'
(Luke 11:41)

Research

Find out if your church or other local churches are working with the homeless, or research local charities that you could get involved with.

Pray

Jesus, help me to have your heart of compassion for the lost and broken.
Help me to find opportunities to serve them and demonstrate your love.
Amen.

Reaction Reaction Reaction Reaction

CIRCLE:

☺ ☹ 😐 😮 😕 😲

TICK:

Total rubbish ☐   Not sure ☐   Worth thinking about ☐   Genius ☐

FILL:

....
....
....
....

Living on Peanuts

Chip talks

I've always found the story of George Washington Carver extremely inspiring. He was born into slavery in 1864, but after slavery was abolished in America, George found himself in possession of a peanut farm. He prayed, asking God to show him how he might possibly be able to make a living out of peanuts, and by the time of his death in 1943 he was a recognized and established scientist, botanist, educator and inventor . . . all because of peanuts!

G eorge Washington Carver's life serves as an enduring testament to God's ability to take someone living in complete poverty and turn their life around for good. History teaches us that people of all walks of life are capable of rising up from a place of poverty, and the Bible teaches us that God doesn't play favourites. **IF HE CAN DO IT FOR GEORGE, HE CAN DO IT FOR THE REST OF US.**

There were eight 'cardinal virtues' that George Washington Carver compiled for his students to strive towards:

- **Be clean both inside and out**
- **Neither look up to the rich nor down on the poor**
- **Lose, if need be, without squealing**
- **Win without bragging**
- **Always be considerate of women, children and older people**
- **Be too brave to lie**
- **Be too generous to cheat**
- **Take your share of the world and let others take theirs**

Choose today to not only rise above the poverty mindset yourself, but to bring others with you. Remember that it can only be accomplished in the strength God provides. Jesus says that apart from him we can do nothing, but with him all things are possible.

God's Word says:

'I will give my followers a long life and show them my power to save.'
(Psalm 91:16)

You let our enemies run over us. We went through fire and water, but you brought us to a safe place.
(Psalm 66:12)

Jesus looked at them and said, 'For people it is impossible. But God can do anything.'
(Matthew 19:26)

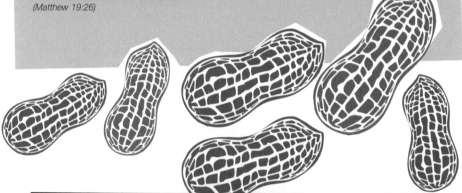

Reaction ReactionReactionReaction

CIRCLE:

☺ ☹ 😐 😮 😕 😲

TICK:

Total rubbish ☐   Not sure ☐   Worth thinking about ☐   Genius ☐

FILL:

....

....

....

....

Hungry?

Helen talks

We can sometimes think that hunger and poverty only affect people in faraway countries like Africa or India, but actually the number of households in the UK in poverty is on the rise. The Trussell Trust is a UK charity that has set up hundreds of foodbanks, which served almost 350,000 people with emergency food parcels in 2012–13 alone. This was a massive increase on the numbers they served in the previous year. That is, people in the UK who were going hungry because they didn't have enough money to buy food. Doesn't that seem a bit crazy? In a country where many of us spend £30 or more a month just on our phones and media or entertainment or £2.80 every time we buy a coffee, there are people who are too poor to buy food.

Whose responsibility is it to sort things like this out? The government? The local council? The local schools? What's really exciting about the foodbank movement in the UK is that local churches are taking responsibility for feeding the hungry in their own neighbourhoods. It's the Christians who are getting involved in lobbying Parliament to address the issues of hunger in this nation and lending practical support to people in need.

We often hear in the media that the Church is dying, people are leaving, that Christianity is no longer relevant and is on the decline. WHAT BETTER WAY IS THERE TO DEMONSTRATE THAT GOD IS ALIVE, RELEVANT AND INTERESTED THAN FEEDING THE HUNGRY? Sometimes it is hard to see how the Church can really address the massive needs we see in society but it only takes a few people to start a movement that can have a nationwide impact. Churches are uniquely placed to be able to set up and run food banks. Most churches have lots of volunteers, links into local communities and are trusted by people. Who knows what other needs we could also be meeting as we show God's love to a hurting world.

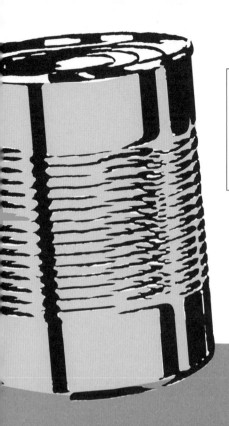

Consider

- What are your unique skills and gifts?
- What circumstances has God placed you in where you can use those gifts to help, support or inspire others?

Read

- 2 Kings 4:42–44
- Matthew 14:13–21

Reaction ReactionReactionReaction

CIRCLE:

😊 🙁 😐 😮 😏 😲

TICK:

Total rubbish ☐   Not sure ☐   Worth thinking about ☐   Genius ☐

FILL:

....

....

....

....

Reality Check

POVERTY FACT FINDER

How much do you know about the poor people in the world? Take some time to research and top up your knowledge. To get you started, type in POVERTY FACTS to an Internet search engine. Look through some of the websites and find answers to the questions below. Some useful websites might be:

www.unmillenniumproject.org

www.endpoverty2015.org

www.oxfam.org.uk

Poverty

What are some of the causes of poverty?

1..

2..

3..

4..

How many people in the world live on less than $1 per day?

....

Hunger

How many children die every year as a result of hunger?

....

How many people go to bed hungry every night?

....

Health

What are some of the main diseases that affect the poor around the world?

1...

2...

3...

4...

What percentage of the world's population don't have basic water sanitation?

..................%

Education

How many adults in the developing world are illiterate?

....

What percentage of them are women?

....................%

Get involved

Like us, you might have been shocked by some of the facts you have discovered. You might feel helpless against such huge problems. What can one person do?

Well there is an African proverb that says, 'Anyone who thinks they are too small to make a difference has never spent the night with a mosquito!' You can make a difference. Use these facts to inspire you to pray, give and do your part to help combat the giants of poverty and hunger.

World Injustice

I also saw these things in this life:

I saw that the courts should be filled with

goodness and fairness, but there is evil there now.

(Ecclesiastes 3:16)

First up

How amazing is the Bible?! The verse you've just read from Ecclesiastes could be something you find on a Christian Aid, Oxfam or Make Poverty History website today, even though it was written thousands and thousands of years ago. Think about all the things that we have done and developed since those words were written by a king in the Middle East — we've been to the moon, invented electricity, we have mobile phones, the Internet, communication, massive advances in health care and food production and yet nothing has really changed. There is still evil where there should be justice. There is still wrong instead of right.

Underneath all the technology and information we are pretty much the same as people were thousands of years ago. We still try and get something for nothing, we still look out for number one, we still want more and more for ourselves. Did you know that there is enough food produced in the world to feed everyone in it and yet 800 million people go to bed hungry every night? Isn't that crazy?!

Things aren't fair. We in the West live privileged lives and although we don't always see the direct link, our blessed lifestyle is often directly linked to someone else's suffering. We know it's not something that's easy to fix, we can't just send all our leftovers to Africa and make it all OK. There are so many incredibly complex issues that very clever and powerful people wrestle with every day and struggle to find answers to. However, we know that if we all learn more, take more personal responsibility and get involved we can make a difference.

This Life Lesson will help you learn more about some of the issues that are out there; it's not always easy reading, but take some time to find out where evil exists instead of good and think about what you can do to make a difference.

Me, Me, Me

Luke 12:16–21

A rich industrialist had had an excellent year and got an enormous bonus. He thought to himself, 'Just how am I going to spend this? I work so hard that I am perfectly justified in spending this on myself.'

Then he thought, 'I know what I will do. I will buy another large house in the country just in case I ever get a day off. I will furnish it with expensive ornaments and the most extravagant furnishings I can buy. I will purchase a new top-of-the-range convertible with my own personalized number-plate. I could even afford a private jet. This would be very useful because I am such an important person and it would help me to get around all my businesses more quickly. Then I will be able to look around and say to myself, "Look at what I have achieved." I have got so much here, I really will be able to enjoy myself in the years ahead. One day, I keep promising myself, I will take life easy. I will eat, drink and be merry.'

The man lived like a fool. He lived just for himself. He lived as if this life would go on for ever. But that night he died. So who now is going to get all the things he had so selfishly stored up for his future use?

The message of this story is clear. This is how it is going to be for everyone who hoards things for themselves and ignores God's teaching and the desperate needs of others.

While many people struggle through life barely managing to survive, others seem to coast along effortlessly. To them life is a doddle – everything smells of roses, everything they touch seems to turn to gold. Life will always be like this. They haven't a care in the world . . . Then they die.

How do you feel when you read that the 300 richest people in the world have more accumulated wealth than the poorest 50% of the entire world's population? Or even worse, that **THE 3 RICHEST PEOPLE IN THE WORLD HAVE MORE WEALTH THAN THE 48 POOREST COUNTRIES? IS THIS RIGHT?** We are so privileged, but it could just as easily have been you and me starving in one of those 48 countries, desperately looking to our brothers and sisters in Christ in prosperous countries such as the UK to do something about it.

We need to be aware of these facts and then we need to do something positive about it. Not paying lip service to this, but living as simply as we can and giving as generously and as often as we can. This is not communism. This is unconditional love in action.

Keith Tondeur, *Street Parables*, Authentic Media, 2004

ReactionReactionReactionReaction

CIRCLE:

☺ ☹ 😐 😛 😕 😮

TICK:

Total rubbish ☐   Not sure ☐   Worth thinking about ☐   Genius ☐

FILL:

....
....
....
....

Hidden pearls

 When I read my paper I see that there are some very rich people in the world and I think that's wrong. I think there ought to be a limit. It's wrong that one person should have that much money when there's so much need. Even in poor countries there are some very rich people at the top controlling everything, but the money isn't spread out to the poor.

OPPRESSED on all sides

Some would say these are some of the saddest verses in the Bible:

> Again I saw that many people are treated badly. I saw their tears, and I saw that there was no one to comfort them. I saw that cruel people had all the power, and I saw that there was no one to comfort the people they hurt. I decided that it is better for those who have died than for those who are still alive. And it is even better for those who died at birth, because they never saw the evil that is done in this world.

(Ecclesiastes 4:1–3)

The reality of these verses came home to me on 19 May 2004. I remember the date because it was the day that my beautiful niece Hannah was born. I was anxiously waiting for news from the hospital, as it had been a far from simple labour. To kill time, I flicked through various TV news channels and I couldn't believe my eyes. In the space of just one hour, an Iraqi wedding near the Syrian border was bombed (killing around forty people), a march in Gaza was bombed (killing around the same number), Tony Blair was hit by a condom full of purple paint during Prime Minister's questions, Rudy Guiliani was being heckled by 9/11 victims' families at the 9/11 inquest and American generals were trying to explain what had happened at Abu Ghraib to a Senate committee. I thought, 'What kind of world are we welcoming you into, my little one? I am so sorry that we couldn't get things better tidied up for your arrival. I would fully understand if you never wanted to come out.'

The tears that I saw that day are merely a drop in the ocean of the 'tears of the oppressed' all over this planet. There are many people and organizations who are trying to comfort the oppressed today, but there are many more that still have 'no comforter'. Pray about what 'comforting' role God may call you into. It may be physically in another

country, or it may be by giving financially to an organization like Tearfund. Visit their website today: www.tearfund.org.

Sometimes the only way to help the oppressed is to confront their oppressor. Check out the work of the International Justice Mission, who physically remove those caught up in forced and bonded labour all over the world, especially those being used as sex slaves: www.ijm.org.

Derek Kidner, in his book on Ecclesiastes, closes with

these sobering words: 'While we, as Christians, see further than he (the author of Ecclesiastes) allowed himself to look, it is no reason to spare ourselves the realities of the present.'

Andy Flannagan, *God 360°***, Spring Harvest and Authentic Media, 2006**

Reaction Reaction Reaction Reaction

CIRCLE:

☺ ☹ 😐 😐 😌 😲

TICK:

Total rubbish ☐   Not sure ☐   Worth thinking about ☐   Genius ☐

FILL:

....

....

....

....

The Big Issue

Luke 16:19–31

There was a rich young man who worked in the City. He always wore the latest fashions and lived in absolute luxury every day. Outside his office was a poor man, Dave, who tried to earn a living by selling copies of the Big Issue. He was very poor and his only friend seemed to be his dog, which would sit with him and keep warm on winter days.

One day the Big Issue seller died and found himself in the luxury of heaven. The rich man also died and had an elaborate funeral. In hell, where he was in torment, he looked up and saw God far away with the

Big Issue seller by his side. So he called out, 'Father God, have pity on me and send that chap to dip the tip of his finger in cold water and cool my tongue, because I am in agony down here.'

But God replied, 'Son, remember that in your lifetime you received your good things, while this poor young man had next to nothing. But now Dave is comforted here and you are in endless agony. And beside all this, there is a great chasm between us that cannot be crossed one way or the other.'

The rich man replied, 'If this is true then please, God, send someone to my father's house on earth, because I have a large family and none of them believes this to be true. Let somebody warn them so at least they will not have to enter this place of endless torment too.'

God replied, 'But my Son died for them. It is also written in the Bible. They need to pay heed to all the signs that are already so clearly spelled out.'

'That's no good,' the rich man replied. 'They think like I used to do, that this is all a load of rubbish. But now I know it's true. If you were only to send someone from the dead or give some other miraculous sign, I am sure they would radically alter their views.'

But God said to him, 'If they will not believe the evidence that is all around them, if they will not even believe the words of my beloved Son Jesus, they will never be convinced – even if someone was raised from the dead they would try to explain it away!'

It's not ours!

The condemnation of accumulation of great wealth is one of the most regularly repeated messages of Jesus' ministry. **THE GAPS IN OUR WORLD BETWEEN RICH AND POOR ARE OBSCENELY LARGE**, so this teaching needs ramming home to comfortable decadent Christians in the West as never before. This enormous gap between rich and poor is not condemned in our churches – it is mirrored in them. We can criticize the desperate single mum buying a lottery ticket, but we see nothing wrong in spending thousands on private health care for ourselves. (After all, there is nothing wrong with wanting the best for ourselves, is there?)

This story is, however, not a new message just for today's materialistic society. We have always had the tendency to want to keep things for ourselves. Church fathers have tried through the ages to address the issue. Augustine said, 'To succour the needy is justice.' Ambrose said, 'You are not giving the poor person the gift of a part of what is yours. You are returning something to him which is really his.' Chrysostom said, 'Do not say, "I am spending what is mine." It is not actually yours. It is someone else's.' Basil said, 'It is the hungry one's bread you keep, the needy one's money you have hoarded.' And Jerome said, 'All riches originally derive from injustice.'

Are you beginning to get the picture? Every time I read this parable I feel very uneasy. In fact, I need to share something with you. As I started to work on his parable, I was all ready to condemn the rich young man for his uncaring nature when a little voice inside my head pointed out to me that I was no different. **WHAT WAS I DOING PERSONALLY TO IMPROVE THE LOT OF PEOPLE LIKE DAVE?** As a result of this, I went through a period when I was unable to write a word. It lasted more than three months. So if you ever feel there is a finger pointing at you, I can assure you that there are at least three pointing at me.

Keith Tondeur, *Street Parables*, Authentic Media, 2004

Reaction Reaction Reaction Reaction

CIRCLE:

😊 🙁 😐 😮 😌 😲

TICK:

Total rubbish ☐ Not sure ☐ Worth thinking about ☐ Genius ☐

FILL:

....
....
....
....

Everyday Choices

Chip talks

When it comes to issues of world injustice, it's easy to shift the blame. After all, we're not responsible for things like tsunamis or corrupt government officials or sex trafficking or underpaid, overworked bricklayers in India. It's even easier to shift the responsibility for dealing with these issues of injustice. Surely that's something for our world leaders to take care of, right?

Or is it?

B elieve it or not, choices that you make every day could affect the livelihoods of other people who are going about their daily routines somewhere on the opposite side of the world. The places you shop, the products you buy, the websites you visit and even the way you treat the environment all have knock-on effects that may go further than you realize. For instance, the chocolate bar you ate last week probably came from a factory not very far from where you live, but the ingredients of the chocolate itself may have come from a plant farmed in South America by workers who are forced to live and work under the most strenuous conditions, with little to no pay. And all you were concerned with was whether or not the chocolate would give you spots!

There are loads of contributing factors to the unjust treatment of human beings. Selfishness, envy, lust, laziness and hatred can all ultimately find their root in GREED. That's why the Bible says that 'the love of money causes all kinds of evil' (1 Timothy 6:10). **AND IF WE'RE HONEST WITH OURSELVES, WE'RE ALL GUILTY OF SOME FORM OF GREED.** We like to take shortcuts. We want to make more money and work less. We want our business to be profitable, even if it's at the expense of others in our industry. And all of this leads to injustice of one kind or another.

So maybe there *is* something we can do. Maybe we can shop fair trade. Maybe we can sponsor a family living on the other side of the world. Maybe we can write to our MPs about human trafficking. Maybe we can treat others the way we would like to be treated.

Jesus travelled to Nazareth, the town where he grew up. On the Sabbath day he went to the synagogue as he always did. He stood up to read. The book of Isaiah the prophet was given to him. He opened the book and found the place where this is written:

'The Spirit of the Lord is on me.
He has chosen me to tell good news to the poor.
He sent me to tell prisoners that they are free
and to tell the blind that they can see again.
He sent me to free those who have been treated badly
and to announce that the time has come for the Lord
to show his kindness.'

Jesus closed the book, gave it back to the helper, and sat down. As everyone in the synagogue watched him closely, he began to speak to them. He said, 'While you heard me reading these words just now, they were coming true!'

(Luke 4:16–21)

ReactionReactionReactionReaction

CIRCLE:

☺ ☹ 😐 😮 🙂 😲

TICK:

Total rubbish ☐   Not sure ☐   Worth thinking about ☐   Genius ☐

FILL:

....

....

Hidden pearls

We should always try and stop corruption and stand up for laws that are right.

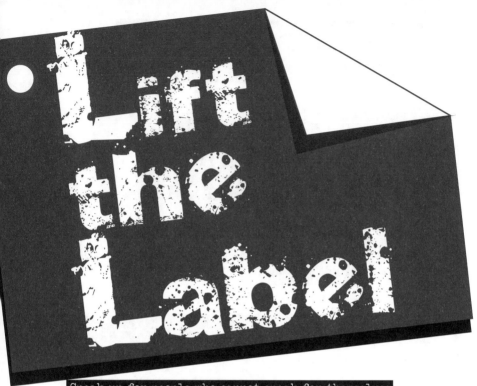

Lift the Label

(Proverbs 31:8)

Check the labels of the clothes you are wearing (perhaps as you're putting them on). Where are they from? The likelihood is that they have been manufactured somewhere in South-East Asia. Feed your discoveries through to the website. In Bangladesh I saw 'Made in Germany' and 'Made in the USA' labels being sewn onto clothes. I also saw the conditions that many garment workers have to work in, and you definitely handle your clothes differently when you realize how many hands have actually touched them before you. Many workers in Bangladesh receive less than £5 a week. They would need twice that amount to be able to afford basic essentials like food, healthcare and accommodation. This is the case for millions of clothing industry workers around the world.

P rofits are being put before people – and many workers (90% of whom are women) are trapped in the cycle of poverty as a result. Add to this the horrendous conditions in many of the factories and . . . well, how are your clothes feeling on you right now?

A great way to get involved is by joining Tearfund's 'Lift the Label' campaign. They are calling on UK clothes retailers to join the Ethical Trading Initiative, asking companies to take responsibility for ensuring that the people making the clothes they sell work in safe and healthy conditions, are paid a wage they can live on, have the right to organize themselves into trade unions and speak out to improve conditions. Add your voice today via www.tearfund.org/youth then follow the links.

This is a fantastic way to quite literally **SPEAK UP FOR THOSE WHO CANNOT SPEAK FOR THEMSELVES.** In terms of the global market economy, their voices are the quietest whisper compared to our booming voices, so we must make ourselves heard.

Pray for God to lead you to other voiceless people in our society and in the wider world who you could 'speak up' for.

Peopletree (www.peopletree.co.uk) and No Sweat Apparel (www.nosweatapparel.com) have built up great reputations for fairly traded clothes.

Andy Flannagan, *God 360°*, Spring Harvest and Authentic Media, 2006

Reaction ReactionReactionReaction

CIRCLE:

☺ ☹ 😐 😮 😕 😲

TICK:

Total rubbish ☐   Not sure ☐   Worth thinking about ☐   Genius ☐

FILL:

....
....
....
....

Name: **Kerri Hughes**

Age: **14**

Town: **Nantwich**

Occupation: **Student and part-time gymnastics coach**

If you could change the colour of fire what would you change it to?

Pink

And the colour of your sister's teeth?

Black

If you sneezed with your eyes open, do you really think your eyes would pop out?

Yeah, maybe.

How old were you when you found out Santa wasn't real?

I think I was about 7. I was gutted.

Who do you identify as 'hungry' people – which nations?

Africa, India and Asia.

Is there such a thing as spiritual poverty?

Yes, because poverty is when you've got no home. You've got nothing. Spiritual poverty is having no religion, no one to follow, no meaning in your life.

Gated Communities

Helen talks

Chip and have I just got back from a holiday in South Africa, visiting my sister who lives there. I was so excited because I've wanted to go ever since I was 17. When I was doing Geography A level we used to watch videos about South Africa and I know I was supposed to be concentrating on the socio-political problems and geographical things like that, but I just kept thinking that it looked like a really cool place to visit. So it was amazing to finally go there. We had a great time, and I definitely recommend it.

B eing over there got me thinking about colour and class and integration and all that stuff. In the UK we have a fairly integrated way of life, with people of all colours and religions able to live fairly similar lives. In South Africa this is totally not the case. Because of Apartheid (an old system of government which favoured the whites and seriously disadvantaged blacks – if you want to learn more just type 'South Africa Apartheid' into a web browser or go old-school and look it up in a book), it seemed that most basic, menial jobs were done by black people and most professional jobs were done by whites. It was quite obvious that white people had more money than most black people. For example, all the people working in restaurants were black and those sitting down eating were white; all the people begging or selling knick-knacks at traffic lights were black and all those driving in air-conditioned cars were white. I found it a bit of a culture shock and found that, as a white person, it made me feel guilty that, because of an injustice done to them in the past, many black people just did not have the opportunities that white South Africans, or you or me in the West, have today. **WHILE THINGS ARE SLOWLY CHANGING, HISTORY IS STILL HAVING AN IMPACT ON LIFE TODAY.**

Another thing that struck me was that many of the white people live in gated communities. These are like housing estates but with high walls all round the edge and guards on the door to make sure only the 'right' people are let in. These estates were gorgeous – proper MTV *Cribs* kinds of places – with swimming pools, Jacuzzis, the lot. But down the road there were townships with thousands of black people living in shacks with no running water or electricity.

To start with I felt a bit judgemental of those white people who, instead of trying to work towards integration and a better, fairer society, were just locking themselves away and trying not to see all the poverty and dirt in the country. It was as if they were saying, 'As long as I'm alright, that's all that matters.' But just as I was judging those white people for their separation and small-mindedness, I realized that I do exactly the same thing. We all do the same thing. I realized that the UK is really just a massive gated community. We put up walls, and border control, and have immigration laws, and try to keep the world's poor people out.

Many people in the UK are worried that the refugees and asylum seekers coming in from other countries will take 'our jobs', 'our benefits' or 'our school and hospital places'. People think they should just go home. The truth is, many refugees have fled for their lives. Often they leave behind family, good jobs and their own culture, and they come to the UK as a desperate last resort. Think about it. You wouldn't leave your home and everything you know and love, with nothing but a suitcase, then travel, cramped in the back of a lorry for days, risking death, if you weren't really desperate. At the end of the day, there is injustice in the world, and many people do not have the advantages and opportunities in life that we have. Many have been treated unfairly by their leaders or by world leaders. **LET'S MAKE SURE WE DON'T JUST PUT UP THE WALLS AND HOPE THAT WE WILL BE OK.** Let's make sure we are getting involved, trying to help, being aware of all the poor people just outside our 'community'. Take some time to find out more about asylum seekers and refugees in this country, and perhaps you will see that a lot of the prejudices people have against them are untrue. Check out www.refugeecouncil.org.uk to find out more.

ReactionReactionReactionReaction

CIRCLE:

😊 ☹️ 😐 😦 😕 😮

TICK:

Total rubbish ☐   Not sure ☐   Worth thinking about ☐   Genius ☐

FILL:

....

....

Third World Debt

Part of the reason such a large gap exists between rich nations and poor nations is because of debt. Loads of the poorest countries owe the rich countries (and western world banks) loads and loads of money. Lots of these loans were given out in the 1970s and 1980s and not always to the best people or for good reasons. Since the loans were given, many poor countries have found the value of their own currencies decreasing against the value of the US dollar, which most of the loans are in. This means that, in reality, the loans are much bigger and harder to pay back. Increases in interest rates have also made the loans even bigger. Many of these loans were given to dictators or bad governmental regimes that didn't even use the money for the good of the people who are now paying them back. Lots of poor countries spend more on paying back their debts than they do on road building, health care, education and agriculture put together! There are many people campaigning to change this situation and already billions of dollars of debt have been cancelled. Find out how you can get involved in a practical way by checking out www.jubileedebt.org.uk or www.wdm.org.uk. Just by signing a petition or finding out more, you are already making a difference.

ReactionReactionReactionReaction

CIRCLE:

😊 ☹️ 😐 😮 🙁 😲

TICK:

Total rubbish ☐   Not sure ☐   Worth thinking about ☐   Genius ☐

FILL:

....

....

Good News to the Poor

I have been to many churches that meet on council estates. I've walked past homes and listened to the cries of a mother screaming at her child to get out of her sight. I've seen graffiti covering every wall with obscene pictures and comments, the aftermath of a Saturday night strewn across the roads – broken bottles, takeaway packets, syringes all over the place. Destruction and disillusionment abound.

One church I visit meets right in the middle of such an estate. Large cars line the car park, and a security guard is hired to protect the congregation's property. I press the buzzer to announce my arrival and am allowed to enter once I have been vetted. I walk into the sanctuary as the organ strikes up the first traditional hymn. The congregation is made up entirely of white, middle class, middle-aged and elderly people, most of whom travel a fair distance to worship here every Sunday. Another church greets me with a cartoon poster of a stereotypical burglar in a black and white top and swag bag swung over his shoulder. Beneath his picture a caption reads: 'Beware, non-members about!' No-one from the estates surrounding these two churches attends the meetings. I don't stop to wonder why.

William Temple (Archbishop of Canterbury, 1942–44) once said, **'THE CHURCH IS THE ONLY INSTITUTION THAT EXISTS FOR THOSE WHO ARE NOT YET ITS MEMBERS.'**

Jesus declared that he was not here for the righteous but for sinners: 'Sick people are the ones who need a doctor, not those who are healthy' (Matthew 9:12). Yet so often our churches are dedicated to making us feel safe and welcome, forgetting those on the outside who desperately need to hear the Good News.

Often, when discussing the Christian response to social justice our minds run straight to dusty mud huts in Africa, or to the war-torn Middle East. We forget that social justice is just as important, just as necessary, on our very own doorstep.

William Booth didn't forget this. As a Methodist minister his overwhelming desire was to see the lost saved and social reform in Britain. Caring for the homeless, the drunks and the poor at a time when there were no social services, no option of collecting benefits, he resigned his position in the Methodist Church and worked ceaselessly to bring the kingdom of God about in this nation. He established the Salvation Army, which by the time he died was active in fifty-eight countries. It spoke a language that Victorian England understood. No hypocrisy, just straight down the line gospel preaching accompanied by active faith lived out in the community. People flocked to the Salvation Army banner. They flocked to Jesus. 'While women weep as they do now, I'll fight. While little children go hungry as they do now, I'll fight. While men go to prison, in and out, in and out, as they do now, I'll fight. While there is a drunkard left, while there is a poor lost girl on the streets, **WHILE THERE REMAINS ONE DARK SOUL WITHOUT THE LIGHT OF GOD, I'LL FIGHT – I'LL FIGHT TO THE VERY END,'** he said.

We meet people every day who need to know the Good News of Jesus. They need to hear it and they need to be faced with the reality of it in their lives. God cares about the whole person: their soul, their health, their hopes and their hurts. Jesus embodied that fact every day. Today we are being transformed into his likeness. Jesus is with us every day. We are part of the kingdom of God. We are called to bring good news to those that need it.

Andy Frost and Jo Wells, *Freestyle*, Authentic Media, 2005

Reaction Reaction Reaction Reaction

CIRCLE:

TICK:

Total rubbish ☐   Not sure ☐   Worth thinking about ☐   Genius ☐

FILL:

....

....

....

....

LIFE LESSON THREE

Bringing God's Justice

I will tell you the kind of day I want: a day to set people free. I want a day when you take the burdens from others. I want a day when you set troubled people free and you take the burdens from their shoulders.

(Isaiah 58:6)

3

First up

Can you think of a time when you were treated unjustly? I remember once in maths class my teacher accused me of cheating on my homework and I really hadn't. I wasn't much good at maths but I hadn't cheated! I still remember how that felt. The feeling that someone thought badly of me and there was nothing I could do to change it. Now imagine how much worse it would be to be in a situation of injustice where you have to live every day with the results of that injustice.

Imagine you are an Iranian journalist living in Iran and have to flee the country when the government threatens you because they don't like the truths that you print. You are forced to come to the UK with nothing, and your plea for asylum is denied because the British government doesn't believe that your life would be in danger if you were to return home.

Imagine living every day, earning £3 an hour working illegally in a restaurant doing a boring, menial job, all because of an injustice done to you by the Iranian and British governments.

Or, how about this?

Imagine starting your first job. Everything is going great until you get accused of stealing some money from the safe. You know you didn't do it but you don't have an alibi and you end up getting arrested and left with a criminal record. As a result, whenever you go for a job interview you are turned down because you don't have good references.

God sees everything. He sees what really goes on. He is a God of ultimate justice and while we often have preconceived, prejudiced ideas of situations, people groups and individuals, he knows the truth. As Christians we should be helping to bring God's justice on earth. We should be rooting out injustice and uncovering hidden truths, standing up for the marginalized and trapped. That might be in your school, your workplace, your street, your town. Search out injustice and be someone who shines God's justice into the darkness.

RagstoRiches

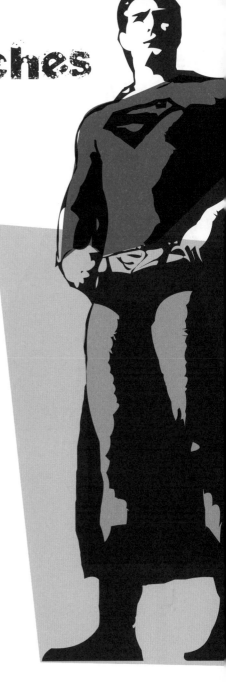

Chip talks

Many people don't realize that the original biblical word for 'righteousness' can also be translated as 'justice'. The two words mean pretty much the same thing – doing what's right, even in the face of opposition. But imagine the implications if we were to read certain Scriptures in the light of this new translation . . .

The Bible says in Isaiah 64:6 that our own righteousness (justice) is like filthy rags, and in Romans 3:10 that not a single person on earth is right (just) 100% of the time. We may try our best, but at some point we'll fall flat on our faces trying to make everything perfect. That's a job only God himself can do.

The Apostle Paul wrote in Philippians 3:9, 'I want to belong to him. In Christ I am right with God, but my being right does not come from following the law. It comes from God through faith. God uses my faith in Christ to make me right with him.' So our heavenly Father literally takes us from rags to riches – the rags of our own justice to the riches of his justice through our faith in Jesus. What a great swap!

When I was a kid, I loved watching Superman, Wonder Woman, Batman, Aqua Man, Flash and other superheroes join forces to become the Justice League.

I wanted to be in that league! But based on what the Bible says about the justice of God (which *isn't* fantasy by the way), I've discovered that he's prepared something far greater for me. I CAN be right with God, literally BE the justice of God in Christ (2 Corinthians 5:21), and wear his justice as a breastplate. That's far better than anything DC Comics could ever offer me.

> So stand strong with the belt of truth tied around your waist, and on your chest wear the protection of right living.
>
> *(Ephesians 6:14)*

Try replacing 'right' with 'just' and 'right living' with 'justice' in these verses too:

Matthew 5:10

Psalm 5:8

Romans 10:3–4

James 3:18

ReactionReactionReactionReaction

CIRCLE:

TICK:

Total rubbish ☐ Not sure ☐ Worth thinking about ☐ Genius ☐

FILL:

....

....

....

....

River of Justice

Here is an exercise for you to try with your youth group or church.

Scripture focus: 1 Samuel 7:2–6

Type of prayer: Intercession

Time needed: 45 minutes

Supplies: a cross – either one that is used in your church worship, or one you make out of pieces of wood (it needs to be quite large to provide a good focal point at the centre of the room); 4 large pieces of card; materials to inform prayers such as newspaper headlines, pictures, names of people who are in need; pens

Overview

Intercession is praying to God for other people – standing in the gap between them and God and bringing their needs before him. This activity illustrates this by getting people to join hands as they pray, forming a human connection between the cross and the need for prayer. By acting out the spiritual reality and physically bridging the gap between God and the need, it reminds people of what they are doing and helps them grasp the significance of their prayers.

Set-up

You will need an empty room. Set up the cross in the middle of the room. Decide on four things that you want to encourage people to pray about – perhaps people who are ill or in need, people who don't know Christ, situations of conflict around the world and situations of need in the neighbourhood. Set up a 'station' for each of these – one on each of the four walls of the room. Each station should be a piece of card stuck on the wall with a title telling people what to pray about and some inspiration for prayer stuck around it such as pictures, words, newspaper headlines and so on. Put some pens under the board so that people can write up their own ideas for prayer. Experiment to see how many people are needed to link hands and form a human chain between the cross and each station and this will tell you how many people need to be in each small group.

The Idea

Ask people to sit on the floor around the cross. Explain what the word intercession means – standing in the gap between God and someone in need and bringing that need to God in prayer. Explain that this activity will enable people to spend some time in intercession, praying for people and situations in need.

Invite people to go round the room, visiting each of the four stations in turn, identifying needs for prayer at each and writing them up on the card. Allow about fifteen minutes for them to do this.

Now comes the actual prayer. Illustrate how this will work with a few people, hold hands in a chain so that one person touches the cross and the person at the other end touches the wall. The person next to the cross prays first for the need on their heart and then each person in turn prays. If people are not used to praying out loud in front of others, they can pray silently and then say 'Amen' aloud to indicate when they have finished. Allow plenty of time for people to move around the room and pray. After 20 to 25 minutes, or earlier if people are running out of steam, tell people they have one more minute in which to finish their prayers. After that minute call everyone together and lead them in thanking God that he has heard their prayers and will answer in his way and in his time.

Jenny Baker, *Transforming Prayer*, Spring Harvest and Authentic Media, 2004

ReactionReactionReactionReaction

CIRCLE:

TICK:

Total rubbish ☐   Not sure ☐   Worth thinking about ☐   Genius ☐

FILL:

....

....

....

....

Name: **Diana Mukasa**

Age: **20**

Town: **London**

Occupation: **Student**

PEOPLE CLIP

Favourite song

'Hosanna' – Israel Houghton

Favourite passage of Scripture

Jeremiah 29:11: 'This message is from the LORD. "I have good plans for you. I don't plan to hurt you. I plan to give you hope and a good future."'

Where's the strangest place you've ever woken up?

University campus

If you could change the colour of grass what would you change it to?

Yellow

And the sea?

Purple

If you were Prime Minister for a day, what would you change?

Laws in media: what information is fed to our generation. And injustice: feed the hungry – those who were born without the option to eat.

Jesus turned the world upside-down by never doing or saying what was expected of him. Israel was waiting for a Saviour. They had been under foreign rule for centuries, and under Roman occupation since 63 BC. They were an utterly oppressed nation clinging to the promise of God that he would send someone to set them free.

 esus declared that he was the one that they had been waiting for. But he was not going to be some great warrior king. He was going to die for freedom, not fight for it.

WE MUST OBEY GOD, NOT YOU

Politically, Jesus was playing a dangerous game. As God's ambassador, he was sent to complete the Scriptures and declare Israel as God's chosen nation. But God's agenda has always been bigger than that. God wants the whole world to be in a relationship with him. So to release the oppressed meant far more than doing so for the nation of Israel only.

Perhaps the easiest way to understand this is to look at one of the challenges the Pharisees made to Jesus that we read about in Matthew 22:15–22. They set a trap for him, asking whether Jews should pay taxes to the Romans. They were asking whether Jesus would support the oppression of the Jewish people by financially supporting the oppressor. Surely God would say it was wrong? But it was a double trap because the Pharisees brought with them allies of the Romans so that if Jesus were to say that it was wrong, he would be arrested for treason. **IT WAS A NO-WIN SITUATION. EITHER HE SUPPORTED OPPRESSION OR HE RISKED IMPRISONMENT.**

Jesus replied, 'Give to Caesar what belongs to Caesar, and give to God what belongs to God' (Matthew 22:21). His answer

Oppressed

was that justice and freedom would come through God, not futile arguments.

Isaiah 1:17 says, 'Work for justice. Help those who suffer under the control of others. Speak up for the widows and orphans. Argue for their rights.' God never supports social and economic oppression. His heart is always for freedom. But throughout the Bible, we are told to pray for our persecutors and to honour those in authority. In Romans, Paul tells us to submit to those in authority as God gives them their authority over us. However, we read in Acts how **JOHN AND PETER REFUSED TO STOP PREACHING ABOUT JESUS, EVEN WHEN IT BECAME ILLEGAL.** Their argument was 'We must obey God, not you' (Acts 5:29).

So what should we do when on the one hand we are told to honour those in power, whilst on the other we are told to obey God, not man, and defend the rights of the oppressed? There have been varying views about what it is to defend the rights of the oppressed. They range from the so-called 'permitted violence in liberation theology' to the apathetic 'tut-tut!' found in many evangelical churches.

A few years ago a family of Kosovan asylum seekers got deported illegally from our community. One minute they were round at our homes playing football with us. The next minute they were gone, no warning, just tears in the aftermath. Should we have just shrugged our shoulders and sighed, 'What a shame'? Should we have stormed the Houses of Parliament with machine-guns and demand them back? No. Instead we did the only thing we could do – we pleaded their case.

WORK FOR JUSTICE

STAND UP TO THE BULLIES

We kicked up the biggest fuss we could. We marched in protest, we spoke to newspapers, radio and TV stations. We raised money for lawyers and we went to court. We did not stop until our case was heard. Our government had mistreated those it should have helped and we were going to fight until it was put right.

Politicians asked us to be quiet. But we would not be quiet. **WE WERE SPEAKING ON BEHALF OF THOSE WHO COULD NOT SPEAK FOR THEMSELVES.**

After eight months the Home Office admitted their mistake one week before our court case was to be heard. Within six days the family were home.

Silence lies at the heart of oppression. The oppressed are unable to speak for themselves. Christians are charged with the responsibility to speak up for them. Prejudice and persecution is rife in our society. Poverty, alternative lifestyles, religious beliefs, nationality, all lead to people suffering needlessly in life. Oppression is simply a fancy word for bullying. We need to stand up to the bullies, shower them with grace and pray for the conviction to change.

Andy Frost and Jo Wells, *Freestyle*, Authentic Media, 2005

ReactionReactionReactionReaction

CIRCLE:

TICK:

Total rubbish ☐   Not sure ☐   Worth thinking about ☐   Genius ☐

FILL:

....

....

Hope for Justice

Ben talks

Imagine being taken from your family against your will. Kept as a prisoner, you are forced to beg on the streets, work long hours for no pay or sell your body as a prostitute. When you try to escape you are beaten. Every night you cry yourself to sleep, praying that one day someone will help you.

This is real life for millions of young people across the world who are victims of human trafficking. Some are used as slave labour or forced to become child soldiers, others are abused in the sex trade. Traffickers are criminals who buy and sell people and then exploit them to make money. Human trafficking is a global problem and many countries including the UK are affected by it.

The facts

- **1.2 million children are trafficked every year**
- **The average age of a trafficking victim is just 14 years**
- **It is estimated that $9.5 billion is made through human trafficking each year**
- **2,255 potential victims were identified in the UK in 2012**

Think

'The Spirit of the Lord GOD is on me. The LORD has chosen me to tell good news to the poor and to comfort those who are sad. He sent me to tell the captives and prisoners that they have been set free.'
(Isaiah 61:1)

1. Is it our job as Christians to stand up against injustice? Why?

2. What other issues of injustice do you see in the world that you feel strongly about?

What can I do?

Human trafficking is a massive problem and many people think there is nothing they can do to help. The truth is that you can make a difference!

Hope for Justice is an organization that exists to rescue victims of human trafficking – modern day slaves – and aims to inspire and equip a generation to get involved in the fight for justice. Read on for some ideas to help you get involved.

Careers

There is a desperate need for more social workers, lawyers and investigators to work alongside charities and organizations that rescue people and bring traffickers to justice. Maybe you could consider one of these as a career choice. Or if you want to work in politics you could influence others in government and speak out on behalf of vulnerable people.

Start an ACTFORJUSTICE group

ACTFORJUSTICE groups meet every month to pray, campaign, fundraise and receive the latest news on trafficking from Hope for Justice. It's a great way to join the Hope for Justice community. Why don't you think about starting an ACTFORJUSTICE group with friends in your area?

Pray

Prayer can change situations and it is a powerful weapon in the fight against human trafficking. Ask God to give you his heart for trafficked people and pray regularly for organizations who are working to bring freedom to those in slavery.

Give

Consider making a donation to or raising money for a charity working to rescue people from human trafficking.

Go Deeper

The word injustice means that someone is unfairly treated or their rights are violated. There are many different kinds of injustice. This includes a wide range of issues, from the terrible treatment of trafficked people to someone being bullied at school, or being treated badly because they are poor or of a different nationality.

1. Write down three ways you could act against the injustice you see in your school, workplace or community.

....
....
....
....

2. Write down two ways that you could get involved in fighting human trafficking.

....
....
....
....

For more information about human trafficking or ACTFORJUSTICE groups visit the Hope for Justice website at www.hopeforjustice.org.uk and click 'Take Action'.

Ben Cooley
www.hopeforjustice.org.uk

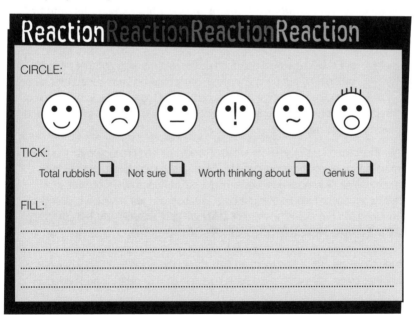

Reaction Reaction Reaction Reaction

CIRCLE:

TICK:
Total rubbish ☐   Not sure ☐   Worth thinking about ☐   Genius ☐

FILL:

....
....
....
....

Is the Really Grass / Greener

Helen talks

Throughout the world there are Christians living in areas of hardship and injustice in countries where war rages, dictators rule, freedom is limited and ordinary people's lives are a struggle. Edward Kajivora is a Christian living in South Sudan, the world's newest country. He works with the Bible Society and, despite enduring terrible hardship, is committed to staying where he is to provide support and help to others in his community. He could flee like many people in the region have and avoid the gunfire, possible kidnappings and violence. Edward recently said, *'I am still in Juba and decided to remain for two reasons. First, death is everywhere and when your time comes, you cannot escape. Second, as a priest I have been assigned to help a small congregation not far from my house. I felt I should be among them to encourage them with the comforting word of God. I tell them that nothing can separate us from Christ.'*

For Edward it would be much easier to jump ship and get himself to a safe place, but he is choosing to sacrifice his own comfort for others. Sometimes the best way we can bring God's justice is by standing firm in a hard situation, keeping on doing right, living by godly principles and trusting him for everything.

Are there situations in your life where it would be easy to look over the fence to someone else's situation and say, 'Hmm, the grass looks greener over there, I think I'll jump the fence.' It might be someone else's church, job, family, school or friends. It might be a situation you are in which challenges you to stand out as a Christian. **IT CAN OFTEN BE APPEALING TO TRY SOMETHING NEW INSTEAD OF STANDING FIRM.** Occasionally, like in Edward's case, the grass might actually be greener in another place, but even then God can still call us to stand firm. Often the grass isn't really greener in another place, it's just that we have become tired or disillusioned with our

on the Other Side?

current circumstances. Standing firm means keeping working, keeping on singing, keeping on trusting God, showing that in any situation God is there. Sometimes we need to remember that if we are there, then God is there and can use and bless the best and the worst situations.

Think

Are there any situations in your life where you are considering jumping the fence because the grass seems greener somewhere else? Pray about whether God is calling you to stick where you are.

Research

There are loads of organizations that help support people in Edward's position, people who are subject to war or injustice or persecution. To find out more you could research the Bible Society, Open Doors and Amnesty International.

Reaction ReactionReactionReaction

CIRCLE:

TICK:

Total rubbish ☐   Not sure ☐   Worth thinking about ☐   Genius ☐

FILL:

....
....
....
....

The Social Gospel

LOVE THY NEIGHBOUR

About 100 years ago there was a big split in the Church. On the one hand people were arguing that the call of a Christian was to love their neighbour. They argued that people would come to know Christ through us 'embodying' the Gospel. Other Christians argued that the Gospel must be preached; ensuring eternal salvation was the primary task of the church – all other actions were secondary. That led to the big divide we are faced with today. Love in a social context versus preaching the Word.

B iblically, however, the two were never meant to be separated. The Gospel is about living as a community that personifies the kingdom of God and it's about the relationship available for us as individuals to be children of God. Peter commands us to live such good lives that people will ask us about our life choices (1 Peter 2:12). Paul commands us to preach the Word (2 Timothy 4:2) – that we are to proclaim the name of Jesus at all times. Both camps were right – but somewhere along the line things got forgotten. Or maybe things just go too hard.

There can be an attitude that 'proclamation evangelism' is the most important aspect of the Christian life. That God only really cares about people's spiritual situations. And anyway, it's too hard to try and change their physical situation. Billions of dollars of debt, war rife around the world, dirty politics on both sides, and Joe Bloggs gets stuck in the middle. **YOU CAN SEE WHY IT'S OFTEN EASIER TO TALK ABOUT SALVATION IN HEAVEN RATHER THAN THE KINGDOM OF GOD BEING ESTABLISHED ON EARTH.** But our God promises to move when we share his heart for justice. The task is huge, but if you look throughout history you will see that God has honoured that promise. Insignificant people who have faith in a completely powerful, totally sovereign God, have dared to believe that they can move the mountain of injustice and send it crumbling into the sea. Dare we believe it too?

Andy Frost and Jo Wells, *Freestyle*, Authentic Media, 2005

PREACH THE GOSPEL

Reaction Reaction Reaction Reaction

CIRCLE:

☺ ☹ 😐 😲 🙂 😮

TICK:

Total rubbish ☐   Not sure ☐   Worth thinking about ☐   Genius ☐

FILL:

....
....
....
....

Reality Check

TAKE A STAND FOR JUSTICE

Look up the dictionary definition of injustice and fill it in below. (If you don't have a dictionary, try www.dictionary.com.)

....

....

....

....

....

Write down an example of an injustice that is happening right now that you CAN'T do anything about:

....

....

....

....

....

....

....

....

....

....

....

Now pray for that situation. If you want you could also fast. Fasting is when we give up something to show God how serious we are about whatever it is we're praying for. It could be food, TV, talking – anything. Instead of doing those things, spend the time in prayer.

Now write down an example of an injustice that is happening right now that you CAN do something about.

....

....

....

....

....

....

....

How can you help bring God's justice into this situation?

....

....

....

....

....

....

Now go and do it. If you want you can write how you got on in the space below. Make sure you pray for that situation too.

....

....

....

....

Get Involved

My dear brothers and sisters, you are believers in our glorious Lord Jesus Christ. So don't treat some people better than others. Suppose someone comes into your meeting wearing very nice clothes and a gold ring. At the same time a poor person comes in wearing old, dirty clothes. You show special attention to the person wearing nice clothes. You say, 'Sit herein this good seat.' But you say to the poor person, 'Stand there.'or 'Sit on the floor by our feet.' Doesn't this show that you think some people are more important than others? You set yourselves up as judges – judges who make bad decisions.

Listen, my dear brothers and sisters. God chose the poor people in the world to be rich in faith. He chose them to receive the kingdom God promised to those who love him. But you show no respect to those who are poor. And you know that the rich are the ones who always try to control your lives. They are the ones who take you to court. And the rich are the ones who insult the good name of your Lord, the one you belong to.

My brothers and sisters, if a person claims to have faith but does nothing, that faith is worth nothing. Faith like that cannot save anyone. Suppose a brother or sister in Christ comes to you in need of clothes or something to eat. And you say to them, 'God be with you! I hope you stay warm and get plenty to eat,' but you don't give them the things they need. If you don't help them, your words are worthless. It is the same with faith. If it is just faith and nothing more – if it doesn't do anything – it is dead.

(James 2:1–7, 14–17)

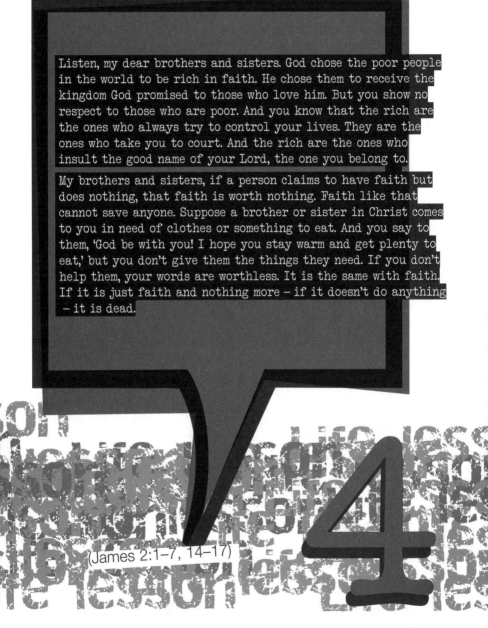

First up

We were going to write a bunch of stuff for this 'First up', but we realized that what you've just read in James chapter 2 already said it!

As Christians we need to get involved. It's not enough just to say the right things and pray the right prayers – we have to actually help the poor. We don't know what that will mean for you – for each person it can be in a different way. Use your creativity. Use the opportunities God gives you – but whatever you do, make sure that you don't look down on the poor. Don't just have faith with no action.

Action

chipK's mind

Have you ever been so annoyed, disturbed and upset by a certain situation that you just *had* to do something about it? It's called 'being provoked to action'. One example might be getting up in the middle of the night to turn off a dripping tap that's keeping you awake. Another might be giving money to a charity after feeling sorry for some starving children you've seen on television. Still another might be even more drastic, like dedicating your life to finding the cure for cancer after watching a loved one battle with the dreadful disease.

I was provoked to action after a certain visit to Manchester's very own shopping paradise, The Trafford Centre. It was a school holiday and I'd heard there was a pop band performing in the food court, so I found my way there and manoeuvred myself through the packed crowd as close to the front as I could get. As it turned out, the band was only fronting a famous modelling company, and they were touring various shopping centres telling young girls how to stay healthy and look pretty. Fair enough. But then they did something that shook me to the very core. They got five young girls onstage and offered a prize to the one who could best mimic the extremely over-the-top sexual dance moves from a music video featuring prostitutes. When those vulnerable, innocent girls proceeded to copy the filth, move for move, in front of a crowd of all ages, I JUST WANTED TO SCREAM, 'NO!' AT THE TOP OF MY LUNGS. Instead I went straight to the information desk and filed a formal complaint. But it wasn't enough. That day, I decided that the vision of Innervation – setting up bands like thebandwithnoname all over the country promoting the Gospel and Christian values – was no longer just a good idea. It was an absolute necessity.

Take a few minutes to pray and think about what provokes you. Could God be calling you to do something about it?

God's mind

There in the Temple area he saw men selling cattle, sheep and doves. He saw others sitting at tables, exchanging and trading people's money. Jesus made a whip with some pieces of rope and forced all the sheep and cattle out of the Temple area. He turned over the tables of the money traders and scattered their money. Then he said to those who were selling pigeons, 'Take these things out of here! Don't make my Father's house a place for buying and selling!'

This caused his followers to remember these words written in the Scriptures: 'I am filled with anger when people dishonour your Temple!'

(John 2:14–17)

A person's body that does not have a spirit is dead. It is the same with faith – faith that does nothing is dead.

(James 2:26)

You should use every opportunity you have for doing good, because these are evil times.

(Ephesians 5:16)

Remember this: there are some terrible times coming in the last days. People will love only themselves and money. They will be proud and boast about themselves. They will abuse others with insults. They will not obey their parents. They will be ungrateful and against all that is pleasing to God. They will have no love for others and will refuse to forgive anyone. They will talk about others to hurt them and will have no self-control. They will be cruel and hate what is good. People will turn against their friends. They will do foolish things without thinking and will be so proud of themselves. Instead of loving God, they will love pleasure. They will pretend to honour God, but they will refuse the power that helps us truly honour and please him. Stay away from these people!

(2 Timothy 3:1–5)

Your mind

What provokes me to action?

....

....

Why does this affect me so much?

....

....

Who do I know who has dedicated their life to solving something that provoked them?

....

....

What is the biggest problem on earth today?

....

....

How can I help solve it?

....

....

Chip Kendall, *The Mind of chipK: Enter at Your Own Risk*, Authentic Media, 2005

ReactionReactionReactionReaction

CIRCLE:

TICK:

Total rubbish ☐   Not sure ☐   Worth thinking about ☐   Genius ☐

FILL:

....

....

He's Calling You

Bible bit

The LORD's message came to me: 'Before I made you in your mother's womb, I knew you.

Before you were born, I chose you for a special work. I chose you to be a prophet to the nations.'

Then I said, 'But, Lord GOD, I don't know how to speak. I am only a boy.'

But the LORD said to me, 'Don't say, "I am only a boy." You must go everywhere I send you and say everything I tell you to say. Don't be afraid of anyone. I am with you, and I will protect you.' This message is from the LORD.

Then the LORD reached out with his hand and touched my mouth. He said to me, 'Jeremiah, I am putting my words in your mouth. Today I have put you in charge of nations and kingdoms. You will pull up and tear down. You will destroy and overthrow. You will build up and plant.'

(Jeremiah 1:4–10)

Shell's bit

A few months after becoming a Christian, this guy that I knew told me that he believed God had put a strong calling on my life to be a healer of broken hearts through music. As a 15-year-old girl I didn't really understand what that meant, so I went home and asked God to tell me more. I was reading through my Bible and reached Isaiah 61:2 and it said, **'HE HAS CHOSEN ME TO COMFORT THOSE WHO ARE SAD.'** I remember feeling a sense of excitement within me and I just knew with all of my heart that God was going to use me to heal people's broken hearts.

A calling is a sense of purpose – a strong urge to spend a chunk of time doing something specific for God. Sometimes God gives us a lifelong calling and sometimes it's a calling for a shorter period of time. Some people have just one calling and some people have a few different callings. It all depends on what God has got for you individually. I've always had one very strong calling, but God has put me in a variety of different jobs and different situations to fulfil that calling.

Look at Jeremiah for example. He was a young boy when God called him to be a prophet to the nations. Jeremiah was scared because he thought he was too young and he was afraid that he wouldn't know what to say, but God promised that he would give him the words to say and that he would be with him at all times to protect him.

When God calls you to do something, he doesn't expect you to know what to do straight away. He just wants you to agree to hold his hand and follow him, trusting that he will teach you and guide you through everything. I hadn't got a clue what it meant to be a healer of broken hearts when God first called me to do it. But over the years God has taught me, equipped me and guided me through it – and even now I'm still learning. Having a calling and being called is just God's way of saying, 'This is what I want to use you for – will you let me?' and then the choice is yours. I know that my calling has taken me out of my comfort zone and it has sometimes been tough, but I've had a goal, an aim, a purpose in my life and it's been a privilege to be used by God in so many ways.

Time to think and pray

- Have you ever felt afraid (like Jeremiah) about what God is asking you to do? If so, have you talked to God or anyone else about it?

- Do you know what God is calling you to do? If you don't, why not try asking God to show you what he is calling you to do? If you already know, how have you started preparing and putting your calling into practice?

Shell Perris, *Something to Shout About Journal*, Authentic Media, 2007

ReactionReactionReactionReaction

CIRCLE:

☺ ☹ 😐 😯 😌 😮

TICK:

Total rubbish ☐   Not sure ☐   Worth thinking about ☐   Genius ☐

FILL:

....

....

Nothing New Under the Sun

> You may be in a place where the poor people are made to suffer
> by those in power. You may see their rights taken away
> unfairly. But don't be surprised! The official who is making
> life hard for them is under orders from another one in a
> higher position. And they are both under even higher
> officials. It is best for a country to have a king in charge
> who will make sure the fields are prepared to produce good
> crops. Those who love money will never be satisfied with the
> money they have. Those who love wealth will not be satisfied
> when they get more and more. This is also senseless.

(Ecclesiastes 5:8–10)

We shouldn't be surprised by institutional sin amongst multinational corporations or governments when we read these verses from thousands of years ago. Often our energies are focused on helping those at the receiving end of injustice, which is good and right, but perhaps we should be focusing more attention on the injustice itself.

In *Rich Christians in an Age of Hunger*, Ron Sider describes an interesting test. Imagine there is a tap filling a bucket of water in front of you. Your task is to stop the bucket overflowing, and you have a teaspoon in your hand. What do you do?

Sadly, many of our efforts to help the poor focus on frantically spooning water out of the bucket. You can help to cut off the tap at source by campaigning for a fairer world economic system, more controls on multinational corporations and greater democracy and accountability in international organizations like the WTO (World Trade Organization) and the IMF (International Monetary Fund).

This is a quote from an editorial of *The Economist*, 2 February 2004:

The selfish pursuit of profit serves a social purpose. And this is putting it mildly. The standard of living people in the West enjoy today is due to little else but the selfish pursuit of profit . . . This is not the fatal defect of capitalism; it is the very reason capitalism works.

On one level they are right – capitalism does work. But without some fundamental restructuring, it only works for the small percentage with capital at the top of the economic pile. If you've bought this book, you're one of those at the top of the pile. Half of the world's population lives on less than $2 a day. There is somebody somewhere suffering as a result of our comfort.

There is not enough space here to get into the detailed arguments of what needs to happen in terms of debt relief and creating a level playing field for developing countries to be able to trade their way forward, but the websites you can access from www.makepovertyhistory.org all provide fantastic information and resources for campaigning.

Help turn off that tap.

Speak (www.speak.org.uk) is a wonderful organization that combines campaigning and prayer. Its campaigns may be focused on national governments, international bodies such as the IMF, or big business.

Get involved.

Andy Flannagan, *God 360°*, **Spring Harvest and Authentic Media, 2006**

ReactionReactionReactionReaction

CIRCLE:

☺ ☹ 😐 😕 😌 😲

TICK:

Total rubbish ☐   Not sure ☐   Worth thinking about ☐   Genius ☐

FILL:

....
....

Hidden pearls

I think as Christians we should help the poor as much as we can. Some volunteer to go and work among them which is even better than giving money.

Darker Sky, Brighter Star

Is there an area or street in your town where house prices are lowest and people would laugh if you even mentioned that you were thinking of moving there? It may be run down, disused, seedy or simply 'the wrong end of town'. You know the sort of place I'm talking about.

It was about that same time that Augustus Caesar sent out an order to all people in the countries that were under Roman rule. The order said that everyone's name must be put on a list. This was the first counting of all the people while Quirinius was governor of Syria. Everyone travelled to their own home towns to have their name put on the list.

So Joseph left Nazareth, a town in Galilee, and went to the town of Bethlehem in Judea. It was known as the town of David. Joseph went there because he was from the family of David. Joseph registered with Mary because she was engaged to marry him. (She was now pregnant.) While Joseph and Mary were in Bethlehem, the time came for her to have the baby. She gave birth to her first son. She wrapped him up well and laid him in a box where cattle are fed. She put him there because the guest room was full.

That night, some shepherds were out in the fields near Bethlehem watching their sheep. An angel of the Lord appeared to them, and the glory of the Lord was shining around them. The shepherds were very frightened. The angel said to them, 'Don't be afraid. I have some very good news for you – news that will make everyone happy. Today your Saviour was born in David's town. He is the Messiah, the Lord. This is how you will know him: you will find a baby wrapped in pieces of cloth and lying in a feeding box.'

(Luke 2:1–12)

God chose the most obscure, private, but degrading surroundings for the most beautiful moment of his union with humanity and then the most public place in the capital city for his most degrading moment. How would you feel if your wedding took place in a car park? Or if your secret sins were exposed all over the tabloid press?

IN WHAT DARK PLACES DO YOU NOT EVEN BOTHER TO LOOK FOR GOD WORKING? Where are the 'stables' of your family, your town or your country? Take some time to think about this. Because you can bet there is a divine presence right in the midst.

Those Christians who work with and among the poor of the world know the truth that the Magi also discovered. You meet Jesus there. In his book *Christianity Rediscovered*, Vincent Donovan talks extensively about our arrogant attitudes with regard to mission. He speaks of our belief that we somehow 'take God' to people, when actually God is already there, and through our interaction we may hope to increase people's awareness of him at work, including our own.

Pray that God would give you some sort of 'bright star' to lead you to these places . . . pray for these places and their inhabitants, asking that they would know the God who is at work amongst them.

Andy Flannagan, *God 360°*, Spring Harvest and Authentic Media, 2006

Reaction ReactionReactionReaction

CIRCLE:

TICK:

Total rubbish ☐   Not sure ☐   Worth thinking about ☐   Genius ☐

FILL:

....
....
....
....

Name: **Tom Naraine**

Age: **20**

Town: **Birmingham**

Occupation: **Student**

What are you studying?

Sports science

Who is the nicest person you know?

Beth, my girlfriend.

If you were re-inventing planet earth, what would you start with?

I'd scrap gravity and just have everyone floating around.

If you were forced to live in a tent for nine months, where would you choose to pitch up?

The beach in Australia.

Tell us one great thing about your girlfriend.

She's pretty!

Is there any justice in the world?

Yes.

What is the greatest injustice?

The spread of wealth. The way it's distributed.

What do you think is the solution?

People need to care a bit more for others, and have the integrity to act.

Materialism

Then the people brought their little children to Jesus so that he could lay his hands on them to bless them and pray for them. When the followers saw this, they told the people to stop bringing their children to him. But Jesus said, 'Let the little children come to me. Don't stop them, because God's kingdom belongs to people who are like these children.' After Jesus blessed the children, he left there.

A man came to Jesus and asked, 'Teacher, what good thing must I do to have eternal life?'

Jesus answered, 'Why do you ask me about what is good? Only God is good. But if you want to have eternal life, obey the law's commands.'

The man asked, 'Which ones?'

Jesus answered, '"You must not murder anyone, you must not commit adultery, you must not steal, you must not tell lies about others, you must respect your father and mother," and "love your neighbour the same as you love yourself."'

The young man said, 'I have obeyed all these commands. What else do I need?'

Jesus answered, 'If you want to be perfect, then go and sell all that you own. Give the money to the poor, and you will have riches in heaven. Then come and follow me.'

But when the young man heard Jesus tell him to give away his money, he was sad. He didn't want to do this, because he was very rich. So he left.

Then Jesus said to his followers, 'The truth is, it will be very hard for a rich person to enter God's kingdom. Yes, I tell you, it is easier for a camel to go through the eye of a needle than for a rich person to enter God's kingdom.'

The followers were amazed to hear this. They asked, 'Then who can be saved?'

Jesus looked at them and said, 'For people it is impossible. But God can do anything.'

Peter said to him, 'We left everything we had and followed you. So what will we have?'

Jesus said to them, 'When the time of the new world comes, the Son of Man will sit on his great and glorious throne. And I can promise that you who followed me will sit on twelve thrones, and you will judge the twelve tribes of Israel. Everyone who has left houses, brothers, sisters, father, mother, children or farms to follow me will get much more than they left. And they will have eternal life. Many people who are first now will be last in the future. And many who are last now will be first in the future.'

(Matthew 19:13–30)

Jesus looks at two problems here: materialism and control.

Jesus always got specific. In this passage he doesn't talk generally about the masses living in poverty across Israel. He brings it down to this rich young man's front door.

it is easier for a camel to go through the eye of a needle than for a rich person to enter God's kingdom

Think

- Do you get incensed about poverty in developing countries?

- Do you think people and politicians should do more to look after the interests of poor nations and not just their own?

- Does it get your goat that in the forty seconds it has taken you to read this section, five children have died of preventable diseases? (Christian Aid)

Steve Adams, *The Word Through Sound*, Authentic Media, 2004

ReactionReactionReactionReaction

CIRCLE:

😊 ☹️ 😐 😲 😕 😮

TICK:

Total rubbish ☐   Not sure ☐   Worth thinking about ☐   Genius ☐

FILL:

....

....

Here I Am, Send Me!

Chip talks

Hopefully you've read something by now in this Life Lesson that has seriously provoked you to some sort of action. We can't be followers of Jesus without following him into the darkest of places, because that is where he calls us to go in order to shine brightly for him. However, I'm very aware that it's always good to balance such an extreme 'call to arms' with a reminder of something else that's very important.

In Matthew 11:28–30 Jesus says these supremely comforting words:

'Come to me all of you who are tired from the heavy burden you have been forced to carry. I will give you rest. Accept my teaching. Learn from me. I am gentle and humble in spirit. And you will be able to get some rest. Yes, the teaching that I ask you to accept is easy. The load I give you to carry is light.'

J esus will never call you to do something he hasn't already prepared and equipped you for. When he died, he cried, 'It is finished!' That was the end of your exasperation, the end of your stress, the end of your striving to accomplish something of worth in your own strength. **HE'S LITERALLY ALREADY FINISHED THE TOUGHEST WORK FOR YOU.** All he invites you to do now is to join him in the great adventure of healing, restoration and celebration. What will your response be? Will you be able to accept his teaching and work from a place of rest?

In Hebrew (the language most of the Bible was originally written in) there is a great word. It's pronounced AH-VOH-DAH. It can mean two things – 'work' and 'worship'. In our modern understanding of these two words, we couldn't think of two more opposite concepts. We tend to think of working as something really difficult that no one really wants to do, and we tend to think of worshipping as something we do when we're singing songs at church. But to the Hebrew mind, these words are one and the same. **OUR WORK IS OUR WORSHIP, AND OUR WORSHIP IS OUR WORK.**

Read Isaiah 6:1–8, and take a moment to look at the example of Isaiah when he received his call from God. Can you honestly make his response your response?

ReactionReactionReactionReaction

CIRCLE:

TICK:

Total rubbish ☐ Not sure ☐ Worth thinking about ☐ Genius ☐

FILL:

....

....

....

....

Reality Check

STEP UP

The title of this Life Lesson is 'Get Involved' and now that's exactly what we want you to do. There are so many ways you can make a difference to the lives of others. Pick one and do it!

Here are some suggestions:

- Go and help out in a soup kitchen or homeless food run
- Give something away to a charity shop
- Get involved with a foodbank
- Stop and talk to a homeless person
- Buy someone who is hungry a sandwich
- Commit to sponsoring a child (www.compassion.com or www.worldvision.org)
- Encourage others in your church to sponsor a child by doing a presentation
- Send a shoe box of gifts through Operation Christmas Child (www.operationchristmaschild.org.uk) or even better get your whole church to do it
- Donate some money to Water Aid or another similar charity (www.wateraid.org)
- Get sponsored to do a run or cycle ride and give the money to a charity
- Set up an ACTFORJUSTICE group with some of your friends (www.hopeforjustice.org.uk)

It is so easy to do something amazing for someone else and often it doesn't even cost anything.

Write down what you have decided to do:

....

....

....

What date did you start?

....

....

....

What surprised you most about the experience?

....

....

....

What did you learn?

....

....

....

What are you going to do next?

....

....

....

Pray

Thank you God for blessing me with everything I have. Please help me to appreciate what you have given me every day. I pray for those who are less fortunate than me. Please protect those who suffer injustice and mistreatment. Please feed the poor, heal the sick and father the orphans. Help me know how I can be your hands and feet on the earth and how I can do all of these things too.

In Jesus' name,

Amen.